Introduction

The youngest of a family of six children, Pam Ayres was born at Stanford-in-the-Vale, Berkshire, during the long cold winter of 1947. Educated at Faringdon, she quickly developed a flair for imaginative writing and drawing, and an intense interest in animals.

Shortly after leaving school, Pam joined the WRAF in order to see some of the world, and spent four years mostly in the Far East and Germany. During a long spell in Singapore, where she had 'something to do with aerial photography', she became active in the local theatre group and developed her love for entertaining others – acting, singing and reciting her poems.

Following her return to England, one of her poems 'The Battery Hen', was chosen by BBC Radio Oxford for inclusion in one of its programmes. This achieved instant acclaim and was subsequently repeated on BBC Radio 4 'Pick of the Week', and eventually on the 1974 edition of 'Pick of the Year'. During this time, Pam made many personal appearances on Radio Oxford and her poems have been broadcast by BBC World Service and CBC Radio Canada.

The big break for Pam came on November 24th 1975 when she appeared on **Hughie Green's 'Opportunity Knocks'** and won the hearts of the viewers who 'voted' her back for a total of four appearances.

Pam Ayres is a natural storyteller and her poems accurately reflect her personality – they bubble along with an innate sense of humour, sometimes born of sheer fantasy, occasionally sardonic, and always bursting to tell a story. Pam's intense feeling for both human and other animals is clearly defined. She has a keen eye for detail and an ability to illustrate graphically with everyday words. Even those poems reflecting a resigned acceptance of the status quo demonstrate an enlightened appreciation of the humorous qualities found within the most desperate situations.

Pam is a 'spinster of the parish' of Witney, in Oxfordshire, where she has lived for the past three years. In addition to her poetry, she is well known locally for her musical abilities on the guitar and ukelele, and makes frequent appearances at all kinds of local functions. When nobody is looking – she goes mountaineering.

Pam Ayres now has a very large following all over the world, and many have likened her work to a 'Breath of Fresh Air'. This book is being published to coincide with the release, by Galaxy Records, of her first LP. I think that you will enjoy them both.

R.G.E.

Madbrains Watkins and his

Madbrains Watkins was his name,
He was a proper cove,
He had a little travellin' fair,
And the roundabout he drove,
He had to wind the handle,
Which he did at such a pace,
That dobs of oil shot off the chain,
And stuck upon your face.

There also was some hawkers,
Who travelled with this fair,
One was a fat Italian maid,
With a lot of hair,
She sold various confections,
From a little row of huts,
And hair got in the candyfloss
And on the monkey nuts.

SOME OF ME POETRY

Pam Ayres

...as seen on "OPPORTUNITY KNOCKS"

Published by:

GALAXY RECORDS
223 Regent Street
London W1R 8TD

Telephone 01-734 9768

Pam Ayres 1st L.P. GAL 6003 is available now from
Galaxy Records, 223 Regent Street, London, W1R 8TD. Telephone 01-734 9768
also available on Cassette GALC 6003

To Jean and Mum

ISBN 0.9504774.0.0.

Travelling Fair

Watkins had another job,
What he did unseen,
At the coconut shy,
Round behind a little screen,
He liked to see his coconuts,
Stuck on good and tight,
So he helped their staying power,
With a little Araldite.

So you could fling them wooden balls,
For all that you was worth,
But you would knock it clean in half,
Before it hit the earth,
Then you might win a goldfish,
In a plastic bag for free,
But the bag would have a puncture,
And bowls was 90p.

There was a row of swinging boats,
And though the ropes was frayed,
Lots of kiddies went on it,
And lots of kiddies paid,
And as their little fisties wrenched,
The boats up in the air,
In his little office box,
Watkins knelt in prayer.

He had a little ghost train,
Where he'd rush out in the gloom,
And as your train went rattlin' by,
He'd hit you with the broom,
Course, if it was old ladies,
He had to take more care,
He'd either grab their knickers,
Or else he'd pull their hair.

He had a fortune teller,
But she only told for men,
Yet blokes went rushin' in that tent,
Time and time again,
When she was tellin' fortunes,
A notice would appear,
Saying: "Don't spend all your money,
Back in half an hour me dear."

So if you sees a travellin' fair,
Come rattlin' down the track,
Make sure Madbrains Watkins,
Is not grinnin' out the back,
Beware of Watkins travellin' fair,
On lovely summer days
Should he declare "You'll walk on air",
He means just what he says.

The Curlers Poem

A set of heated rollers,
Is every maid's delight,
It stops you wearing curlers,
In the middle of the night,
It keeps you looking spick and span,
When all the rest are not,
And though your hands are freezing cold,
Your head, is nice and hot.

The Bunny Poem

I am a bunny rabbit,
Sitting in me hutch,
I like to sit up this end,
I don't care for that end, much,
I'm glad tomorrow's Thursday,
'Cause with a bit of luck,
As far as I remember,
That's the day they pass the buck.

Sam
and the
Paraffin
Man

Sam came home one evening,
The same as all his life,
To find the paraffin man
Had absconded with his wife,
Her coat from off the hanger
And her bootees from the stair
Had vanished, disappeared,
And furthermore, they were not there

He came in through the kitchen,
The place was cold and still,
He tiptoed up the stairs,
In case his missis might be ill,
But nagging doubts they gathered,
Till what really did him in,
Was all across the landing,
He could smell the paraffin.

He took his knuckleduster
And he pressed it on his fist,
He also took a brick
In case the knuckleduster missed,
He set off down the darkened road,
Towards the caravan,
Where he believed his missis
Hugged the paraffin man.

"Oh, the paraffin man, is it?"
Muttered Sam at every stride,
A little bird had told him
How the lorry stayed outside,
How all the neighbours down the street
Joined in the fun and games,
And said with all that oil
Sam's house might well burst into flames.

He came upon the caravan,
His temper running riot,
But even he, had to agree,
The place was very quiet,
But then it quickly dawned on Sam,
This silence was a trick!
So he rushed up to the fanlight,
And he hit it with a brick.

"Come out here with my missis!"
He bellowed at the door,
"I've heard about your lorry,
Parked outside two hours and more"
The caravan door opened,
To reveal a woman's head,
And then a woman's nightdress,
For she'd just got out of bed.

She said "I'm not the paraffin man,
But I am one of his daughters,
You look so worried Sam,
Can I pour oil on troubled waters?"
She beckoned in the caravan,
And Sam stepped up so quick,
Enraptured by her beauty,
He forgot to drop the brick.

Now unbeknown to Sam,
His faithless wife, she had not fled,
But with the paraffin man,
She was hiding in his shed.
She crept up to the window,
Though she had to kneel and crouch,
And saw her husband Samuel
Suffocating on the couch.

She took a pail of water,
And she flung it in the door,
Just for to cool his ardour
Only that and nothing more.
Too late she realised
That it was paraffin she threw,
And they all went up to Heaven,
On a cloud of Esso Blue.

But on a winter's evening,
If your feet are less than quick,
You might smell an oily fragrance,
You might see a ghostly wick,
You might hear the distant rumble
Of a passing caravan,
For things that passion can't ignite,
Paraffin can.

Not you, Basil

Basil he loved Ethel,
    In his heart there burned a flame,
Every night he gripped the sheets,
    And whispered Ethel's name,
He saw her every morning,
    And the breath caught in his throat,
He loved her in her summer dress,
    And in her winter coat.

Each night the lovely Ethel,
    She came to him in a dream,
And lay reclining in the boat,
    He rowed them in, upstream.
Her hand trailed in the water,
    And she was a wondrous sight,
Saying "Basil! I can wait no more!
    Marry me, tonight!"

But his love was unrequited,
    When he saw her every day,
She only said "How do",
    And hurried past him on her way,
To catch the bus to work,
    Where every day from morn to eve,
She gazed out of the window,
    Thinking of her true love, Steve.

Now Steve he ran a scrapyard,
    Once a week he knocked the door,
And Ethel, she would open it,
    Saying "I know what you've come for!
Your rag and bones!" she cried,
    "And here they are, in this here sack,"
And she'd watch with heart a-flutter,
    As he heaved them on his back.

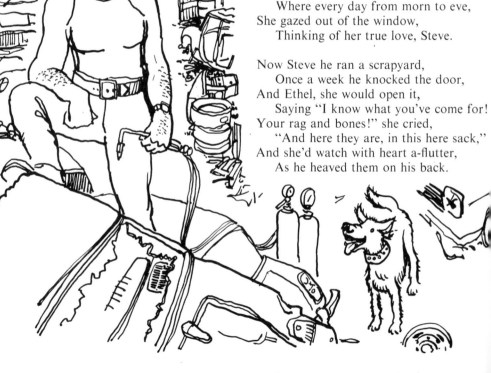

She never thought of Basil,
    Never knew that he was there,
From morn to eve, she thought of Steve,
    Her fingers, in his hair.
For Steve was rugged, like an oak,
    While Basil, like a skittle,
Had no physique, of which to speak,
    His muscles, they was little.

But his ardour never cooled,
    And to himself he sadly said,
"If Ethel do not love me,
    Why, I'd just as soon be dead,
I'll knock upon her door,
    And say 'I love you' and forsooth,
She can either take or leave me,
    But at least I'll know the truth."

So he knocked upon her door,
    And when she answered, he began:
"I know *someone* that you could make,
    A Very Happy Man"
Ethel gripped the doorpost,
    "Do you mean Steve? Oh can it be?"
And Basil, looking at her,
    He said "No, you fool, it's me."

She said "Oh not *you*, Basil
    I thought you'd come on Steve's behalf,
As though he'd see, a girl like me."
    (She laughed a tragic laugh)
She said "I interrupted you,
    What were you going to say?"
And Basil said "Don't matter"
    And he coldly walked away.

Back in his house he primed his gun,
    And placed it to his head,
"I die for Ethel, though my death'll
    Grieve her not," he said.
He strained to press the trigger,
    But his courage upped and fled,
So he rushed out in the garden,
    And he shot the cat instead.

The Frogmarch

This is a story about frogs who each year, in order to breed,
journey back to the pond in which they were hatched. To these
small creatures, motorways are a major obstacle.

Move along the kerbstone there,
And get back into line,
I *know* we've all been sitting here
Since twenty-five past nine,
But I've been doing a traffic census,
And with no more hesitation,
I reckon by tonight,
We'll reach the central reservation.

Now, I don't want my tactics,
Criticised no more today,
I realise that everybody
Knew a better way,
But you are simple country folk,
You do not often come
In contact with these heavy lorries
Rattling down to Brum.

I know that when compared
To boggy river banks and peat,
That M40 motorway
Was murder on your feet,
I also know that in the usual
Places where we sit,
We don't stand up to find
Our underneath stuck up with grit.

Course, life for us amphibians
Is getting very harsh,
Take the Witney By-Pass,
It used to be a marsh,
They've irrigated all the land,
It's all gone to the dogs,
Mind, you get fantastic drainage,
But you don't get any frogs.

Still, keep your wits about you lads,
And before we're very much older,
We'll hop straight in the Promised Land,
And straight off this hard shoulder,
All the female frogs are there,
Tarting up the bower,
I'll give them that, they're very good,
That Sutton Coldfield shower.

Right then, watch the traffic,
'Cause I think I see a gap,
Wake old sleeping beauty up,
With his head sunk in his lap,
Get your bits and pieces then,
Is everybody there?
Look left! . . . Prepare to spring!
Oh No, . . . Here comes St. Giles's Fair.

Honey

My brother was, for many years,
  Apprenticed to the trade,
Of building, and throughout that time
  A million bricks, he laid.
He built a thousand dwellings,
  In bricks of red and brown,
But sometimes, 'fore they built a house,
  They knocked the old one down.

On this partic'lar morning,
  With his companions bold,
He had to knock a house down,
  That was decayed, and old.
The dreaded death-watch beetle,
  He didn't watch no more,
As me brother and his mates they
  Started tearing up the floor.

Well the rafters and the tiling,
  It soon came rattling off,
Then the front door and the windows,
  While the dust it made them cough,
Till at last only the chimney,
  Remained and stood intact,
And the others, to me brother said:
  "You knock that down, we're whacked."

Well first he flexed his muscles,
  And then he flexed his neck,
Then he set about the chimney,
  For to lay it on the deck,
He bashed it in the fireplace,
  And he bashed it in the grate,
And he bashed a bloke stood watchin'
  'Cause he saw him just too late.

But as the fireplace crumbled,
    He was surprised to see,
What come buzzing, panic stricken,
    Out in front of him, a bee.
And where the bricks had fell away,
    Was where it had it's home,
For all lined up the chimney,
    Was a great big honeycomb.

And lovely golden honey,
    It came rolling down the wall,
All in the dust and rubbish
    And the fag ends there and all,
He could not see it go to waste,
    He put the honeycomb,
Into a rubber bucket,
    And he took the bucket home.

Now Mother, she was took aback,
    While staring in the bucket,
"Why thank you dear," she said surprised,
    "All I can say is what luck it,
Was you that knocked the chimney down,
    And brought this home to me,
We'll hang it somewhere warm,
    So's it drips out, in time for tea."

So in the airing cupboard it was hung,
    With bits of string,
And honey ran, into the pan,
    She'd put to catch it in,
It dripped upon the folded sheets,
    And Dad's pants on the rack,
So when he put them on next day,
    They stuck all down his back.

But Oh, it was a luxury,
    With honey on our bread,
When Mother shouted: "Whadya want?"
    "Honey, please," we said,
And in the heated cupboard,
    It gathered in the pan,
As though there was no end to it,
    Out the honey ran.

But Alas! 'twas our misfortune,
    As we found out next day,
We was not the only ones,
    Knew where the honey lay,
Mother, in the morning,
    Went to fetch some for the house,
And found all drownded in the pan,
    Upside down, a mouse!

The honey gummed his whiskers,
    And his fur was stuck up tight,
To add insult on to injury,
    He'd messed in it, from fright,
Mother, with the jamjar,
    She stood at the cupboard door,
Saying "Go and fetch your father,
    There's no honey any more."

Father he ran up so fast,
    His roll-up fell apart,
Saying: "I told you not to put it there!
    I told you, from the start!
I told you we'd get vermin,
    And didn't we get them quick,
Oh, chuck it in the dustbin,
    'Cause it's making me feel sick!"

And so the lovely honeycomb
    Got bundled out the door,
We all went back to Marmite
    Which we used to have before,
My brother searched in vain
    Up every flue his head he put
But he didn't find no more honey
    All he ever found was soot.

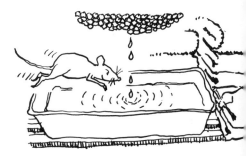

Oh, I Wish I'd looked afte

Oh, I wish I'd looked after me teeth,
   And spotted the perils beneath,
All the toffees I chewed,
   And the sweet sticky food,
Oh, I wish I'd looked after me teeth.

I wish I'd been that much more willin'
   When I had more tooth there than fillin'
To pass up gobstoppers,
   From respect to me choppers
And to buy something else with me shillin'.

When I think of the lollies I licked,
   And the liquorice allsorts I picked,
Sherbet dabs, big and little,
   All that hard peanut brittle,
My conscience gets horribly pricked.

My Mother, she told me no end,
   "If you got a tooth, you got a friend"
I was young then, and careless,
   My toothbrush was hairless,
I never had much time to spend.

...e Teeth

Oh I showed them the toothpaste all right,
    I flashed it about late at night,
But up-and-down brushin'
    And pokin' and fussin'
Didn't seem worth the time—I could bite!

If I'd known I was paving the way,
    To cavities, caps and decay,
The murder of fillin's
    Injections and drillin's
I'd have thrown all me sherbet away.

So I lay in the old dentist's chair,
    And I gaze up his nose in despair,
And his drill it do whine,
    In these molars of mine,
"Two amalgum," he'll say, "for in there."

How I laughed at my Mother's false teeth,
    As they foamed in the waters beneath,
But now comes the reckonin'
    It's *me* they are beckonin'
Oh, I *wish* I'd looked after me teeth.

In Fear of the Butcher

There is an art which ladies have,
With which I can't compete,
And that's the art of knowing
How to pick out joints of meat,
It must be very nice to know
Your sirloin from your rump,
Or if you get a better bet
With brisket than with chump.

You see, me being single,
I never have to care,
A plate of beans and bangers
Will keep me from despair,
But when I have my friends in,
That's when I come unstuck,
That's when I brave the butcher
And go to try me luck.

I stand there in the Butcher's queue
With courage screwed and mustered,
But when I hear "Yes please dear?"
That's when I get all flustered,
That's when I wish I really knew
Me scrag end from me hock,
Me belly from me chitlins
And me knees they starts to knock.

He says "A pound of steak dear?"
(I hates him and he knows it)
Or else he'll say "A chicken?
Here's a fresh one but we froze it."
While all the ladies in the queue
Are shuffling of their feet,
My friends! It is a nightmare
When I buy a piece of meat.

And every single time I say
"I'll have a bit of that!"
Pointing wildly at the window
And a great big lump of fat,
Oh all you other ladies,
I don't know how you do it,
How you acquire what you desire
And not a lump of suet.

I'll be a vegetarian
All gnawing at an apple,
No more with talk of lamb and pork
Will I have to grapple,
And if my friends they visit me,
I'll look them in the eye,
And if they've come to dinner
Well, I'll tell them . . . Goodbye!

I'm a Starling . .

me Darling

We're starlings, the missis, meself and the boys,
We don't go round hoppin', we walks,
We don't go in for this singing all day,
And twittering about, we just squawks.

We don't go in for these fashionable clothes,
Like old Missel Thrush, and his spots,
Me breast isn't red, there's no crest on me head,
We've got sort of, hardwearing . . . dots.

We starlings, the missis, meself and the boys,
We'll eat anything that's about,
Well anything but, that old half coconut,
I can't hold it still. I falls out.

What we'd rather do, is wait here for you,
To put out some bread for the tits,
And then when we're certain, you're there by the curtain,
We flocks down and tears it to bits.

But we starlings, the missis, meself and the boys,
We reckon that we're being got at,
You think for two minutes, them finches and linnets,
You never sees them being shot at.

So the next time you comes out, to sprinkle the crumbs out,
And there's starlings there, making a noise,
Don't you be so quick, to heave half a brick,
It's the missis, meself and the boys!

In Defence of Hedgehogs

I am very fond of hedgehogs
Which makes me want to say,
That I am struck with wonder,
How there's any left today,
For each morning as I travel
And no short distance that,
All I see are hedgehogs,
Squashed. And dead. And flat.

Now. Hedgehogs are not clever,
No, hedgehogs are quite dim,
And when he sees your headlamps,
Well, it don't occur to him,
That the very wisest thing to do
Is up and run away,
No! he curls up in a stupid ball,
And no doubt starts to pray.

Well, motor cars do travel
At a most alarming rate,
And by the time you sees him,
It is very much too late,
And thus he gets a-squasho'd,
Unrecorded but for me,
With me pen and paper,
Sittin' in a tree.

It is statistically proven,
In chapter and in verse,
That in a car and hedgehog fight,
The hedgehog comes off worse,
When whistlin' down your prop shaft,
And bouncin' off your diff,
His coat of nice brown prickles,
Is not effect-iff.

A hedgehog cannot make you laugh,
Whistle, dance or sing,
And he ain't much to look at,
And he don't make anything,
And in amongst his prickles,
There's fleas and bugs and that,
But there ain't no need to leave him,
Squashed. And dead. And flat.

Oh spare a thought for hedgehogs,
Spare a thought for me,
Spare a thought for hedgehogs,
As you drink your cup of tea,
Spare a thought for hedgehogs,
Hoverin' on the brinkt,
Spare a thought for hedgehogs,
Lest they become extinct.

Let's all Strut to the Lifeguard's Hut

It was on the beach at Newquay,
  I was struttin' up and down,
With me bathing suit unbuttoned,
  In the hopes of getting brown,
The icy wind it chilled me
  And the rain washed o'er me face,
But I strutted up and down lads,
  And I never changed me pace.

'Twas then I saw the lifeguard!
  Lyin' flat upon the deck,
A crowd of nubile women,
  Hanging on his words. And neck.
I said "Oh how disgustin',
  Has the man got no decorum?"
For I'd have took his eye lads,
  If I'd just got there beforum.

I strutted on the shingle,
    And I strutted on the sand,
I strutted in the ocean,
    And I strutted on the land,
I strutted through the cafe,
    And I strutted down the rock,
But when it came to struttin' back,
    'Twas then I got a shock.

I had strutted out too far lads,
    And got cut off by the tide,
I could not strut back up the rock
    Nor yet strut round the side
I could not strut upon the ocean
    For sure I could not float
And 'twas then I saw the lifeguard,
    Fast approaching in his boat.

I put my hands up to my mouth,
    And loudly I did call,
As I undid all me swimsuit,
    Rolling up the sleeves and all,
The lifeguard, on the quarterdeck,
    Cried reassuring things,
As he stood beside the tops'l,
    Blowing up his water wings.

Oh I always go to Newquay,
    Yes! I go there each July,
Though I doubt if you would see me,
    Should you chance to wander by,
Nor will you see the lifeguard,
    He'll be in attendance but,
I'll be sheltering from the weather,
    Gettin' rescued, in his hut.

Like you Would

Well I got up in the morning,
Like you would.
And I cooked a bit of breakfast,
Like you would,
But at the door I stopped,
For a message had been dropped,
And I picked it up, and read it,
Like you would.

"Oh Blimey!" I said,
Like you would,
"Have a read of this,
This is good!"
It said: "I live across the way,
And admire you every day,
And my heart, it breaks without you"
Well, it would.

It said: "I'd buy you furs and jewels,
If I could,"
And I go along with that,
I think he should,
It said: "Meet me in the Park,
When it's good and dark,
And so me wife won't see,
I'll wear a hood."

Oh, I blushed with shame and horror,
Like you would,
That a man would ask me that,
As if I could!
So I wrote him back a letter,
Saying "No, I think it's better,
If I meet you in the Rose and Crown,
Like we did last Thursday."

Sling another chair leg
on the fire, Mother

Sling another chair leg on the fire, Mother,
Pull your orange box up to the blaze,
Hold your poor old mittens out and warm them,
In these inflationary days,
Sink your teeth into that dripping sandwich,
Flick the telly on to channel nine,
And if we get the sound without the picture,
Well, I'll kick it in the kidneys, one more time.

Come with me out to the empty garage,
We haven't been there for a week or more,
We'll bow our heads and gaze in silent homage,
At the spots of oil upon the floor.
We'll think of when we had a motor car there,
Which used to take us out in rain or shine,
Before the price of petrol went beyond us,
And we'll make believe we kept it, one more time.

Fling another sausage in the pan, Mother!
We'll laugh away our worries and our cares,
But we'll never get a Doctor after hours Mother,
So for God's sake don't go falling down the stairs,
Toss another lentil in the soup, Mother!
And serve it up before the News at nine,
And if the GPO detector spots us,
Make believe we've got a licence, one more time.

There was a time we'd booked up for Ibiza,
We'd bought the suntan lotion and the clothes,
But we never got beyond the travel agent,
'Cause Court Line organised the one we chose,
So knock the clouds of dust from off the brochure,
Wipe the 40 watt bulb free of grime,
Turn the dog-eared pages to Ibiza,
And we'll make believe we got there, one more time.

Pass me the hatchet and the axe, Mother!
Wipe away that sad and anxious frown,
What with these inflationary spirals,
It's *nice* to see the table falling down,
Your poor old shins will soon be good and mottled,
Once the flames get round that teak veneer,
And in the ring of warm and dancing firelight,
We'll smile and wish each other: Happy New Year.

The Battery Hen

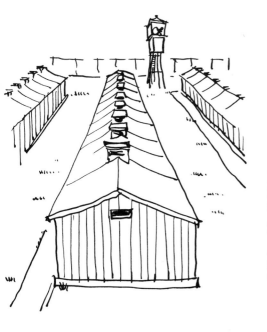

Oh. I am a battery hen,
On me back there's not a germ,
I never scratched a farmyard,
And I never pecked a worm,
I never had the sunshine,
To warm me feathers through,
Eggs I lay. Every day.
For the likes of you.

When you has them scrambled,
Piled up on your plate,
It's me what you should thank for that,
I never lays them late,
I always lays them reg'lar,
I always lays them right,
I never lays them brown,
I always lays them white.

But it's no life, for a battery hen,
In me box I'm sat,
A funnel stuck out from the side,
Me pellets comes down that,
I gets a squirt of water,
Every half a day,
Watchin' with me beady eye,
Me eggs, roll away.

I lays them in a funnel,
Strategically placed,
So that I don't kick 'em,
And let them go to waste,
They rolls off down the tubing,
And up the gangway quick,
Sometimes I gets to thinkin'
"That could have been a chick!"

I might have been a farmyard hen,
Scratchin' in the sun,
There might have been a crowd of chicks,
After me to run,
There might have been a cockerel fine,
To pay us his respects,
Instead of sittin' here,
Till someone comes and wrings our necks.

I see the Time and Motion clock,
Is sayin' nearly noon,
I 'spec me squirt of water,
Will come flyin' at me soon,
And then me spray of pellets,
Will nearly break me leg,
And I'll bite the wire nettin'
And lay one more bloody egg.

The Hegg

A thrush, disconsolate, with no sign of a mate,
Sat morbidly perched in a tree,
Saying "I tell the tale,
Of a flighty young male,
Who have done the dirty on me.

I'm Hexpecting a Hegg, a Hillicit Hegg,
A Hegg lyeth here, in my breast,
While the trees were bright-leaved
I rashly conceived,
A Hegg, Houtside of the Nest.

For my deed I am shunned, and left moribund,
And by all I am left on a limb,
I would give my right wing,
To be rid of this thing,
And for my great girth to be slim."

Just then a black crow, with his black eyes a-glow,
Boldly down to the thrush flew,
Said "The grapevine, I've heard,
Tells of a distressed bird,
Which I've reason to think may be you."

He stood on one leg, said "You're having an Egg,
And the other birds feel you are bad,
But if with me you came,
You'd be free of the shame,
Of having an Egg with no Dad."

"For a nominal fee, I will take you to see,
My friend, who lives up the back doubles,
If you swear not to fail,
To pay on the nail,
He will duff up the source of your troubles!"

So the thrush, unafraid, assented and paid,
And went under cover of night,
To see an old Bustard, with gin and with mustard,
And to be relieved of her plight.

She was made to sit in, a bathful of gin,
And she was obliging and meek,
She was made to consume,
Some soap and a prune,
And her feathers fell out for a week.

Outside on the bough, she said "Look at me now,
Of my Hegg I am freed, but I'm Hill,
And if Hagain I stray,
Without naming the day
Then first I shall go on the Pill."

Pam Ayres and the Embarrassing Experience with the Parrot

At the Cotswold Wild Life Park,
In the merry month of May,
I paid the man the money,
And went in to spend the day,
Straightway to the Pets Corner,
I turned my eager feet,
To go and see the rabbits,
And give them something to eat.

As I approached the hutches,
I was alarmed to see,
A crowd of little yobbos,
'Ollerin' with glee,
I crept up close behind them
And weighed the scene up quick,
And saw them poke the rabbits
Poke them! . . . with a stick!

"Get off you little buggers!"
I shouted in their ear,
"Don't you poke them rabbits,
That's not why they are here."
I must have really scared them,
In seconds they were gone,
And feelin' I had done some good
I carried on along.

Till up beside the Parrots Cage,
I stood to view the scene,
They was lovely parrots,
Beautiful blue and green,
In and out the nestbox,
They was really having fun,
Squawking out and flying about,
All except for one.

One poor old puffed-up parrot,
Clung grimly to his perch,
And as the wind blew frontwards,
Backwards he would lurch,
One foot up in his feathers,
Abandoned by the rest,
He sat there, plainly dying,
His head upon his chest.

Well, I walked on down the pathway,
And I stroked a nanny goat,
But the thought of parrots dyin'
Brought a lump into me throat,
I could no longer stand it,
And to the office I fled,
Politely I began: "S'cuse me,
Your parrot's nearly dead."

So me and a curator,
In urgent leaps and bounds,
With a bottle of Parrot Cure,
Dashed across the grounds,
The dust flew up around us,
As we reached the Parrots Pen,
And the curator he turned to me
Saying "Which one is it then?"

You know what I am going to say,
He was not there at all,
At least, not where I left him,
No, he flit from wall to wall,
As brightly as a button,
Did he squawk and jump and leap,
The curator was very kind,
Saying, "I expect he was asleep."

But I was humiliated,
As I stood before the wire,
The curator went back,
To put his feet up by the fire,
So I let the parrot settle,
And after a short search,
I found the stick the yobbos had,
And poked him off his perch.

The Stuffed Horse

There was a stuffed horse, what had died,
And the townspeople stood it with pride,
On a plinth in the Square,
And the shoppers went there,
And sat, for a rest, by it's side.

Beneath the stuffed horse was a plaque,
Only vandals had painted it black,
What told of the deed,
Of the glorious steed,
And the General, what rode on it's back.

The bold horse with never a care,
Had ducked cannon balls in the air,
And stood to the end,
By the General, his friend,
Which was why he was put in the Sq

Well his tail it was stuck out with wir
And paint, made his nostrils afire,
And his bold eye of glass,
Gazed upon concrete grass,
When he met with his fate, what was

This night from the shadows a-fidget,
Extended a beckonin' digit,
A voice whispered "Right"
And into the night,
Rushed ten men, a saw and a midget.

They lay by the horse with no word,
And the soft sound of sawing was hea
In silence, all night,
Stuffin' flew, left and right,
And into a sack was transferred.

When the church clock struck quarter to four,
Ten men ran away, and a saw,
But the midget, my friend,
Was not there at the end,
He was with his companions no more.

When morning it broke on the Square,
You would never have known they'd been there,
For the horse gazed away,
Like the previous day,
Just sniffin' the Spring in the air.

But walkin' across to the spot,
Came two ladies whose feet had grown hot,
They sat on the ground,
And one got out a pound,
Saying: "Here's that quid I owed to you, Dot."

From the back of the stuffed horse's throat,
Came a hand and it snatched the pound note,
With the hand, and the cash,
The jaws shut, with a clash,
And the horse gazed away with a gloat.

The lady was helped off to bed.
"I thought they liked hay, dear" she said,
No-one listened, of course,
For it was a stuffed horse,
What never required to be fed.

But it happened again, the next day,
When a vicar had sat down to pray,
He said "Lord, bless my flock"
When a great lead-filled sock,
Took his senses, and wallet away.

But by now the long arm of the law
Started pickin' up pieces of straw,
What might have been nothin'
But could have been stuffin'
And random observers, they saw,

That the stuffed horse's eye, though of glass,
Had seemed to be watchin' them pass,
And sometimes would blink,
Or give you a wink,
As if to say "Step on my grass."

Hadrian, of the Yard, he was called,
He was like Fabian, only bald,
He said "I'll be an idiot,
If there's not a midgiot,
Inside of the stuffed horse installed."

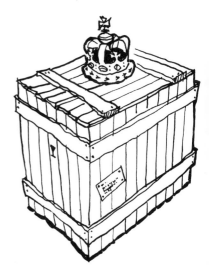

And indeed, that great sleuth, he was right
By Caesarean, they caught him that night,
With ten men and a saw,
He had broken the law
Illegal entry, all right.

But tragic indeed, was the scene,
In the place where the stuffed horse had been,
Bandy legged and defaced,
He had to be replaced,
By an ordinary Bust, of the Queen.

In Favour of Pushing your Car over a Cliff and Buying a Bike

I am a mighty Garage,
On the corner of the Square,
And it is all my pleasure,
To provide a quick repair,
Or I can do your service,
In the blinking of an eye,
I wouldn't say it's thorough,
But it'll get you by.

If you break down, we might tow you in,
I suppose that's what we're for,
Despite the astronomic bill,
It's still a bloody chore,
We'll glare beneath your bonnet,
And we'll reel it off so pat,
Did you know that needs replacing?
And that? And that? And that?

Or we might buy your little car,
For half of what it's worth,
After we've convinced you,
It's got every fault on earth,
But pass me by and presto!
In the window it'll be,
As Clean! One Owner! Spotless!
And the price tag that you see,

Will bear no fond resemblance,
To the price in our demands,
When we said how much we'd give you
Just to take it off your hands,
The price will strangely rocket.
And the things we said were wrong,
Without help from the mechanics
Are conveniently gone!

But when the next poor muggins
He comes looking for a car,
And asks a few odd questions,
They won't get him very far,
We don't say the sub-frame's rotten,
Or the whining from the rear,
Is out of the back axle,
And not ringing in his ear.

For I'm such a busy garage,
And my memory is short,
I don't want people trusting me,
Or troubles of that sort,
We don't want you dissenters,
Butting into our sales pitch,
We just sit here, on the corner,
Growing big. And fat. And rich.

Goodwill to Mer

It was Christmas Eve on a Friday
  The shops was full of cheer,
With tinsel in the windows,
  And presents twice as dear.
A thousand Father Christmases,
  Sat in their little huts,
And folk was buying crackers,
  And folk was buying nuts.

All up and down the country,
  Before the light was snuffed,
Turkeys they got murdered,
  And cockerels they got stuffed,
Christmas cakes got marzipanned,
  And puddin's they got steamed,
Mothers they got desperate,
  And tired kiddies screamed.

Hundredweights of Christmas cards,
  Went flying through the post,
With first class postage stamps on those,
  You had to flatter most.
Within a million kitchens,
  Mince pies was being made,
On everybody's radio,
  "White Christmas", it was played.

Out in the frozen countryside,
  Men crept round on their own,
Hacking off the holly,
  What other folks had grown,
Mistletoe in willow trees,
  Was by a man wrenched clear,
So he could kiss his neighbour's wife,
  He'd fancied all the year.

ive us your Money

And out upon the hillside,
  Where the Christmas trees had stood,
All was completely barren,
  But for little stumps of wood,
The little trees that flourished
  All the year were there no more,
But in a million houses,
  Dropped their needles on the floor.

And out of every cranny, cupboard,
  Hiding place and nook,
Little bikes and kiddies' trikes,
  Were secretively took,
Yards of wrapping paper,
  Was rustled round about,
And bikes were wheeled to bedrooms,
  With the pedals sticking out.

Rolled up in Christmas paper,
  The Action Men were tensed,
All ready for the morning,
  When their fighting life commenced,
With tommy guns and daggers,
  All clustered round about,
"Peace on Earth—Goodwill to Men"
  The figures seemed to shout.

The church was standing empty,
  The pub was standing packed,
There came a yell, "Noel, Noel!"
  And glasses they got cracked.
From up above the fireplace,
  Christmas cards began to fall,
And trodden on the floor, said:
  "Merry Xmas, to you all."

Oh no,
I got a Cold

I am sitting on the sofa,
By the fire and staying in,
Me head is free of comfort
And me nose is free of skin
Me friends have run for cover,
They have left me pale and sick
With me pockets full of tissues
And me nostrils full of Vick.

That bloke in the telly adverts,
He's supposed to have a cold,
He has a swig of whatnot
And he drops off, good as gold,
His face like snowing harvest
Slips into sweet repose,
Well, I bet this tortured breathing
Never whistled down his nose.

I burnt me bit of dinner
Cause I've lost me sense of smell,
But then, I couldn't taste it,
So that worked out very well,
I'd buy some, down the cafe,
But I know that at the till,
A voice from work will softly say
"I thought that you were ill".

So I'm wrapped up in a blanket
With me feet up on a stool,
I've watched the telly programmes
And the kids come home from school,
But what I haven't watched for
Is any sympathy,
Cause all you ever get is:
"Oh no, keep away from me!"

Medicinal discovery,
It moves in mighty leaps,
It leapt straight past the common cold
And gave it us for keeps.
Now I'm not a fussy woman,
There's no malice in me eye
But I wish that they could cure
the common cold. That's all. Goodbye.

Printed in England by Oxley Press (Nottingham) Ltd.